Little **BIG** Chats

Families

by Jayneen Sanders

illustrated by Cherie Zamazing

Families
Educate2Empower Publishing an imprint of
UpLoad Publishing Pty Ltd
Victoria Australia
www.upload.com.au

First published in 2021

Written by Jayneen Sanders
Illustrations by Cherie Zamazing

Jayneen Sanders asserts her right to be identified as the author of this work.
Cherie Zamazing asserts her right to be identified as the illustrator of this work.

Designed by Stephanie Spartels, Studio Spartels

ISBN: 9781761160226 (hbk) 9781761160080 (pbk)

NATIONAL
LIBRARY
OF AUSTRALIA

A catalogue record for this
book is available from the
National Library of Australia

Disclaimer: The information in this book is advice only, written by the author based on
her advocacy in this area, and her experience working with children as a classroom teacher
and mother. The information is not meant to be a substitute for professional advice. If you
are concerned about a child's behavior seek professional help.

Using Little BIG Chats

The *Little BIG Chats* series has been written to assist parents, caregivers and educators to have open and age-appropriate conversations with young children around crucial, and yet at times, 'tough' topics. And what better way than using children's picture books! Some pages will have questions for your child to interact with and discuss. Feel free to use these questions and the Discussion Questions provided on page 19 of this book to help you assist your child with the topic being explored. Stop at any time to unpack the text together; and try to follow your child's lead wherever that conversation may take you! So, please, get comfy and start some empowering 'chats' around some BIG topics with your child.

The Body Safety titles should ideally be read in the following order:
Consent, *My Safety Network*, *My Early Warning Signs*,
Private Parts are Private, and *Secrets and Surprises*.
The remaining titles can be read in any order.

Meet the

Little BIG Chats
KIDS

Theodore

Asha

Ardie

Tom

Jun

Jamie

Belle

Lisa

Maisy

Tilly

Maya

Ben

Hi! I'm Ardie.
Today we're learning
about different kinds
of families.

Every family is different.

My family will be
different to your family.

WHO ARE THE PEOPLE IN YOUR FAMILY?

In some families
there are lots
of people.

In other families there may only be 2 or 3 people.

Some families
love big parties.

And some families
love smaller parties.

Some families like bike riding and some families like to go to the beach.

And some families like both!

All families are different and that's okay.

Benny has two mothers
and a cat called Candy.

Marcia has a mother and
a father and five big brothers!

Finn lives with his grandma
and his three little sisters.

Andy lives with his two dads and his big sister, Katie.

They live on a sheep farm.

Mandy lives with her mother in an apartment.

They don't have space for a dog,
so they have a rabbit instead.

I live with my dad and my stepmother and her daughter, Lexie.

But sometimes I live with my mother and my stepdad and his three kids!

All families are different.
And all families are special
in their own way.

DISCUSSION QUESTIONS
for Parents, Caregivers and Educators

The following Discussion Questions are intended as a guide, and can be used to initiate open, age-appropriate and empowering conversations with your child.

This book celebrates diversity in families. And there are so many kinds of families to celebrate!

Page 5
Introduce Ardie. Ask, 'What do you think we are going to learn about in this book today?'

Pages 6-7
Ask, 'Who are the people in your/our family?'

Pages 8-9
Ask, 'Tom has a big family. Who do you think everyone is? Maisy has a smaller family. Who do you think the adults are? Do you have a big family like Tom? Or a smaller family like Maisy? Does your family live close to you or far away?'

Pages 10-11
Ask, 'What does your/our family like to do?'

Pages 12-13
Ask, 'Do you have a pet? Who do you think is the oldest in Marcia's family? Who do you think is the youngest?'

Pages 14-15
Say, 'People live with their families in all kinds of places.' Ask, 'Would you like to live on a farm? Why do you say that? Where would you like to live with your family?'

Pages 16-17
Ask, 'What is an apartment? Would you like a rabbit or a dog?'

Page 18
Ask, 'How is your/our family special?' Note: promote discussion about culture, family rituals, places family members live or come from, where grandparents live or come from, etc.

For more in-depth books on families and diversity, see Jayneen Sanders' children's books 'Who Am I? I Am Me!'; 'No Difference Between Us'; 'You, Me and Empathy'; 'Be the Difference'; 'I'm Calm' and 'Resilience'.

Little BIG chats

A series of 12 little books to help kids unpack BIG topics

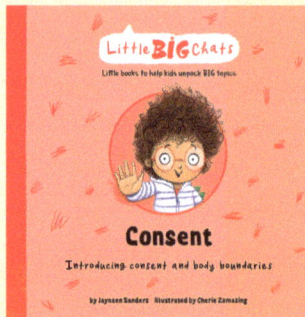

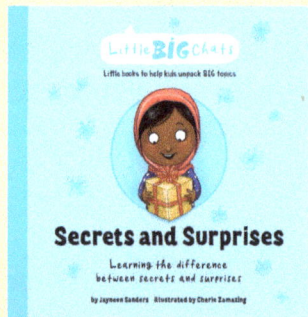

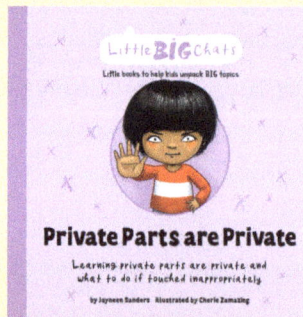

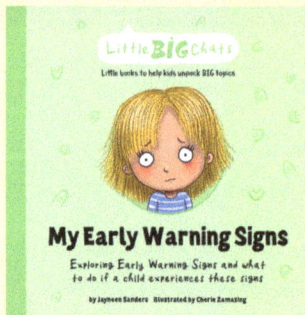

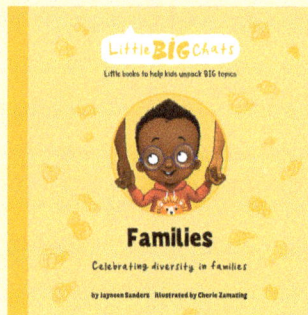

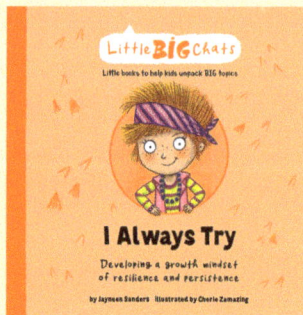

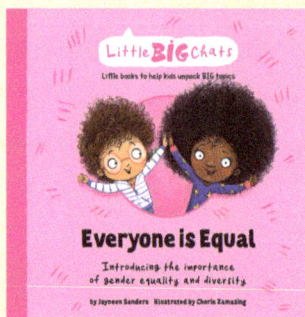

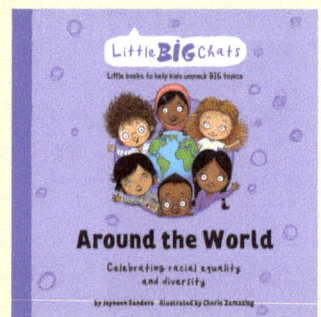

Little BIG chats
Little books to help kids unpack BIG topics
Consent
Introducing consent and body boundaries
by Jayneen Sanders   Illustrated by Cherie Zamazing

Little BIG chats
Little books to help kids unpack BIG topics
Secrets and Surprises
Learning the difference between secrets and surprises
by Jayneen Sanders   Illustrated by Cherie Zamazing

Little BIG chats
Little books to help kids unpack BIG topics
Private Parts are Private
Learning private parts are private and what to do if touched inappropriately
by Jayneen Sanders   Illustrated by Cherie Zamazing

Little BIG chats
Little books to help kids unpack BIG topics
My Safety Network
Introducing a Safety Network (3 to 5 trusted adults a child can go to if they feel unsafe)
by Jayneen Sanders   Illustrated by Cherie Zamazing

Little BIG chats
Little books to help kids unpack BIG topics
My Early Warning Signs
Exploring Early Warning Signs and what to do if a child experiences these signs
by Jayneen Sanders   Illustrated by Cherie Zamazing

Little BIG chats
Little books to help kids unpack BIG topics
Families
Celebrating diversity in families
by Jayneen Sanders   Illustrated by Cherie Zamazing

Little BIG chats
Little books to help kids unpack BIG topics
I Always Try
Developing a growth mindset of resilience and persistence
by Jayneen Sanders   Illustrated by Cherie Zamazing

Little BIG chats
Little books to help kids unpack BIG topics
Feelings
Understanding different feelings and emotions
by Jayneen Sanders   Illustrated by Cherie Zamazing

Little BIG chats
Little books to help kids unpack BIG topics
Everyone is Equal
Introducing the importance of gender equality and diversity
by Jayneen Sanders   Illustrated by Cherie Zamazing

Little BIG chats
Little books to help kids unpack BIG topics
Empathy
Exploring the meaning of empathy and kindness
by Jayneen Sanders   Illustrated by Cherie Zamazing

Little BIG chats
Little books to help kids unpack BIG topics
Mindfulness
Exploring the importance of mindfulness and learning calming skills
by Jayneen Sanders   Illustrated by Cherie Zamazing

Little BIG chats
Little books to help kids unpack BIG topics
Around the World
Celebrating racial equality and diversity
by Jayneen Sanders   Illustrated by Cherie Zamazing